Of a poet
Would you ask
As ask you not
Another?
Of a poet
Would you need
That he would need
To please the needs
You lay to him?
Of a poet
Would you take
For want of taking
Dreams that he could build
For you?
And of a poet
Would you speak
As your own truths
When speaking the words
He spoke to you?
Of a poet—
Of a poet—
That he would answer
And would please
And dream
And lie for you—
You ask it of a poet!

First Printing, March 1973
Library of Congress Card No.: 73-77834
ISBN 0-912310-30-8 Paper Edition
Made in the United States of America

To me!

Publisher's Preface

Bill Harger isn't the greatest thing to come
along in a long time because he doesn't
believe in "greatest." In fact, we're not
sure what he believes in. We know he likes
kids. We know he loves nature. We know
he enjoys people. What we don't know
is when he is speaking of these things,
whether he is serious or trying to be
funny.

Maybe he wants us to smile at our selves
while he twists the blade. In any event,
Bill is not the cynic he sounds to be. He
is positive about life and the unique
beauty of all about, and we are positive
that even though he may not be the greatest
thing to come along in a long time, he is
a long time. Hope you grow to love
yourself in this book. As for Bill Harger . . .
who's Bill Harger?

The first rule
To writing a poem
Is . . . .

Forget all the rules!

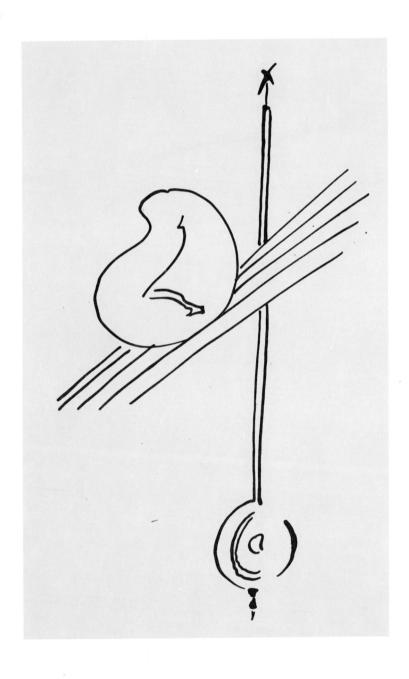

It's time for a new softness,
And it's time for the poets
Across the land
To cry it out,
In softness,
That all our hardened souls,
Well bent to the tasks
We've laid before them
In the history of our folly,
Will cease their futile struggle
To gain what they would gain
At countless other losses.

We must learn to love again,
If love hasn't already
Wrapped herself in drapes of shyness
And silently slipped away
From out our lives completely
And forever,
Into a place of weeping,
Paying the penance
Of her failure to win us over.

We must touch again,
And talk again,
And trust again,
Of one another,
And admit the new softness
Well into our beings,
As it is our only chance
For that which we have
Been seeking
In the years of our searching.
It's time—
It's time—

And it's too late.

What's happening?
I mean,
Where are you going
With your flowers
And your smiles?
I mean,
Could you stop
And rest with me awhile
And share your things—
Your happy things—
Your merry,
Smiling,
Warming things
With me awhile?
Or
Are you on a schedule
That would
Steal them away
From both of us?

Where do ever the frogs
Hide their greeny bodies
When I go looking
For their croak?
And where do all the birds
Singing
Set amongst the branches?
And why can't I
If I choose to cry
Find a place
I'd not be found
Crying?

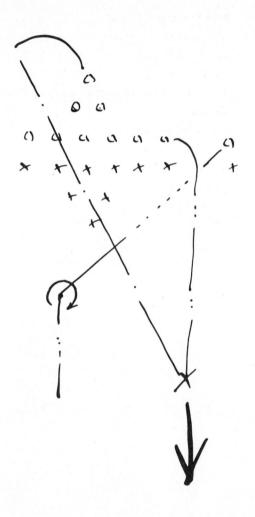

Hey,
I see you
In your broken field
Running form.
You're good.
You're never where they
Think you are
Nor are you
Where you should.
You've analyzed
Most every play
Before the others even knew
There was to be a game.
Yes,
You're good!

At games, anyway.

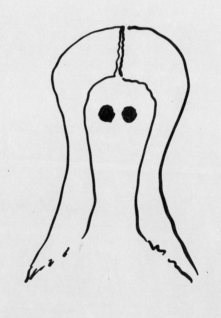

You live your life
The way I want you to
Whether you like it
Or not
Because
You're making mine
Miserable!

When she said she loved me
It was like
No other time I've ever heard
Someone say
She loved me.
When she said she loved me
My heart
Gripped the inside of my chest
As a giant claw
And stole my breath away.
When she said she loved me
My whole self ached
To hold her close to my skin
And feel her full pulse
Beat against my own.
When she said she loved me
The promises
Of all my tomorrows
Lie waiting
In the lap of today
And they were mine
Because she said she loved me.
But
I was twelve
And she was ten
On the day she said she loved me
And I've lost track of her
Since then.

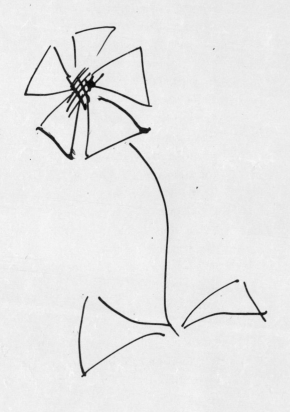

I'm a flower.
Water me I'll grow.
Sun on me
And I'll grow bigger!
Rain on me
And I'm happy.
Snow on me and I'll wilt.
You can do anything to me—
Pick me,
Plant me,
Stamp me,
"He loves me, loves me not" me,
Or put me in a vase.
You can do all these things to me,
But I will remain
A flower
'Cause that's what I am.
You cannot change me.
Nobody can.

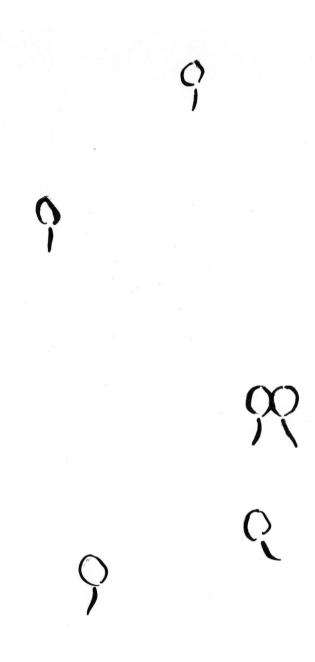

Holding hands
Doesn't really change things.
It just makes them
A little easier to take
In these lonely times.

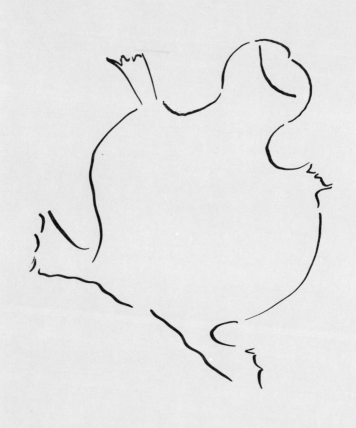

I found a toad
On the drive
The other day,
Out by the turn.
He was squashed,
Of course—
But,
He was still smiling!

William Henderson Haryn I

Why is it—
All poets are philosophers
As well as poets?

They are not—
Poets speak
And everything
Is philosophy
And
Poets speak!

Stop for a moment
And see the changing—
Stop for a moment or so
And see about you,
The little things about you,
Changing,
And think a moment
About the need,
And the beauty,
And the plan
God,
If e're there could be,
And nature
Have placed into being
That all those things changing
Would fit
In a changing scheme.

Stop for a moment
And see those things changing
And wonder at it,
And glory at it
And chance place yourself
In that changing scheme
And change a little too
Or—
Are you perfect already?

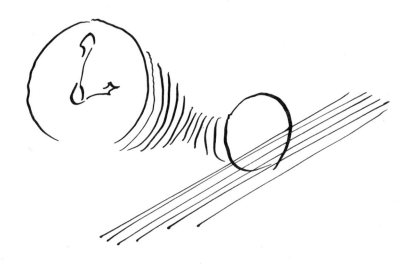

I met an old man
The other day—
Said he was dying.
Now I'm not going to say
I was sorrowful for him,
For his dying I mean,
But
There was something
In the way
He said he was dying
That made me realize
I was too!

Don't I remember you?
It seems to me
You were about as important
As a man could be.
It seems like you were perfect
And had it in the bag.
It seems like you were strong
And the rare epitome
Of all our struggles
To find self
And place
And mental ecstasy.
Weren't you unforgettable?
I swear—
I can't remember.

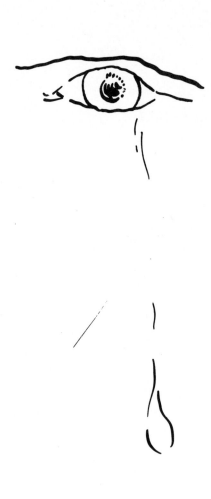

For the people—
A man!
For the people—
A soft
And gentle
And loving
Inspired
Generous
And peaceful man.
For the people—
A man.

Let's get
The son of a bitch!

Do you feel it too,
Or,
Am I the only one?
The rush
Of peace
And dawn
And moist morning air
Dampens my hair
And flushes my cheeks
With the thrill
Of knowing
Where I am,
And why.

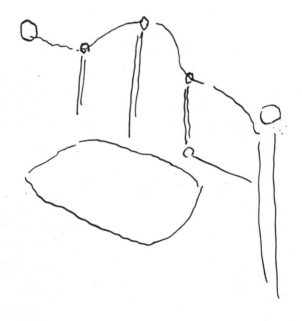

You say you love me
And I say
Bullshit!
There's no such thing
As love
I say.
Just electricity—
An alignment of the poles—
Likes attract likes,
Or positive goes to negative—
Lots of answers
But none for love.
Love isn't!
The flesh thing
Is pleasure.
The heart thing
Is programed.
The tear thing
Is martyrdom.
The lip thing
Is sensuousness.
The sex thing
Is animal.

What!
You want to take me to bed?
But not unless I say
I love you ....

I love you.

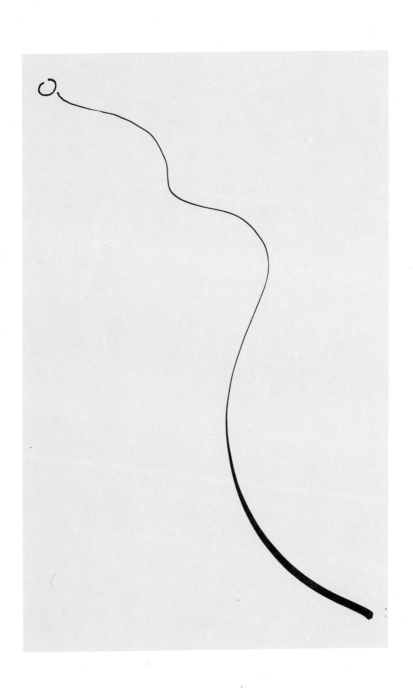

When the moment comes
And you know its yours
Take it
And run with it
And turn it into a lifetime.
Turn that moment
Into a lifetime—
Nobody can stop you.

I love the way you dance around
On my ideas
With your sweet little feet
In circles—
In joy
With me
Singing
Smiling
Hearts aburst with the joy of knowing
The joy of knowing
And flying
Spinning
High above our minds
Out of reach of all those others
And their querious looks.
God I love the way you tippy toe
And spin
And dance around on my ideas
With your sweet little feet.

And you're beautiful too!

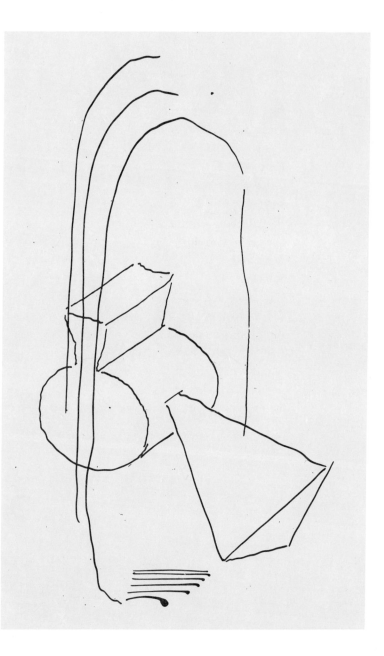

I am my own declaration . . .
My own eternal joy.
I am the things
I've wanted to be
Ever since there ever was me.

In my commune—
—"our" commune,
We don't really help so much
Each other so much.
I'm just there—
—"we're" there
When help is needed
By someone.
But never me.
I never need it.

In my commune—
—"our" commune,
Sex
Isn't the important thing
Everybody thinks it is
In a commune.
Everybody but me,
That is.
All those lovely hunks
Of flesh
Don't impress me at all
The others maybe—
But I never need it.

Yes, my commune—
—"our" commune,
Is a good place
For peace loving,
Forgiving,
And compassionate,
Sensitive,
And humble
People
And I don't want—
—"we" don't want
Any of them
Sex-starved,
Hypocritical,
Plastic society,
Ego maniacs
Around here ...
Them bastards.
This is a nice soft place
And I don't need—
—"we" don't need 'em.

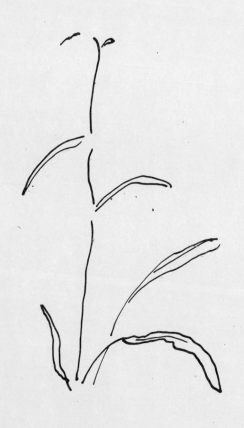

I want to say more
I want to cry
I want to fly
But I'll sit
With my stones
And flowers
And they will pass on
The thoughts I need
To continue.

Well,
Here we go again—
You want to get serious,
And
Talk about truth,
And
Solve your problems,
And
Find happiness.
It's kind of dumb,
Doing this
Over and over again.
Especially since
You're always serious
But don't know the meaning
Of the word—
You find it difficult
To handle any truth
Much less
Any truth about yourself—
You are your own problem
And always have been—
And happiness need not be found.
It surrounds you,
It surrounds us all.
But
I'll probably sit and listen
Anyway.

Occasionally
Your mind is consumed
With a new beginning.
All the thoughts and fancies
Of our yesterdays
Are expurged
In a brilliant crystalline flashing
That thrills your head
And only those thoughts of old remain
That would feel comfortable
In the new thing to happen to you.
And,
At once,
With excruciating
And lonely joy,
You are born again,
Without a host,
Without a conceiver,
Without a nurse,
And without sin
And
God, but it's fine.

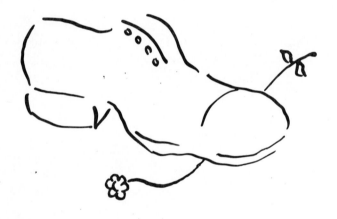

All a man
Really needs from a woman
If he were to be happy
With her
And not command strokes
And pats
And kisses
And certain special duties
And disciplines—
All a man
Really needs from a woman
Is
That she look at him
And say,
With honey in her voice,

"Hey you . . . . C'mere."

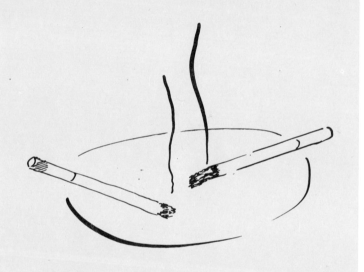

There is the greatest
Possibility
That love isn't.
If it were
That I should love you,
In the way we have known
All love should be
Because we named it so,
Everyone would talk,
And sure,
Even hate be spawned
By the action of our loving.
I have seen it happen—
I have seen it cripple—
I have seen it sour
Minds and souls once sweetened
By the honey touch of love.
I have never
Seen the time
When love did not destroy
Either of the lovers
Or the lover's lovers.
Love isn't,
Or this wouldn't be so.

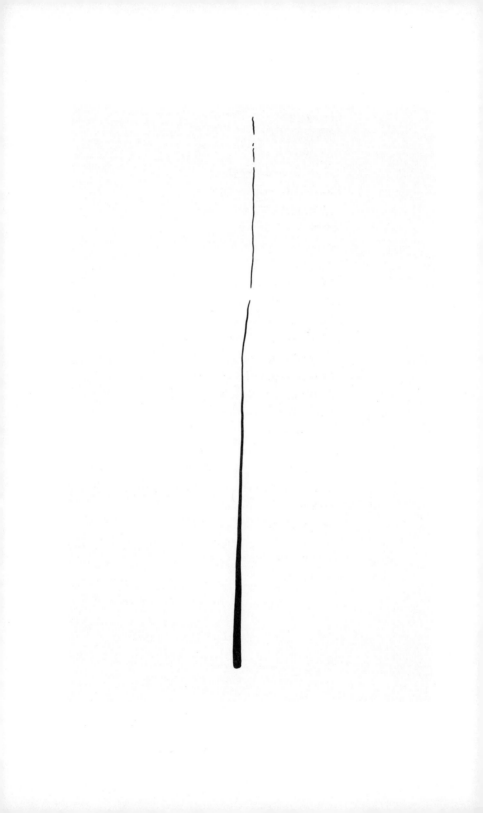

You have yet
To see the day
That lights the way
You have yet to see.

You have yet
To feel the love
That warms the soul
You have yet to feel.

You have yet
To know the strengths
Inside
The despairing human form
You have yet to know.

You have yet
To do the things
That are only yours to do
And yet
Have yet to do.

Yes,
You have yet to do
Anything beyond
What you think you are
And what you think
You need to be.

You don't know
You're the secret
To your existence;
You're the secret
Of your own joy
And so
You copy
And compare
And idealize
And rationalize
All your little lies
To truths
And declarations
Of your vinyl being
And through it all
Hear not the screaming,
Fearless,
Perfect call . . .
You have yet to happen.
You have yet to be.
You have yet to know,
And feel,
And love
The beauty and the wonder
That you,
And only you,
Happen to be.

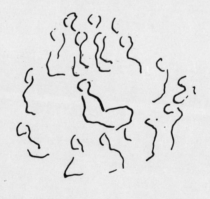

A fellow
Asked me one day,
"Why do you like kids?"
I replied—
"I like kids
Because
When you tell them the truth
They reward you,
And love you,
And want you.
If
You tell the truth
To an adult,
He gets uptight,
Calls you a bastard,
And walks away."
He looked at me a minute,
Called me a bastard,
Turned,
And walked away.

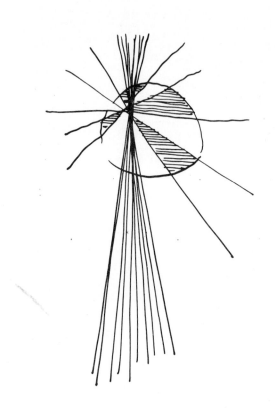

Out of the shadows
Of the minds we cherish
Rush the questions
We charge ourselves
To answer,
But we won't,
Because we cherish our minds
And putting your mind down
Is too high a price to pay
For peace
And truth
And love
And faith
And friends
And communion
And freedom
And warmth
And wisdom
And happiness
And goodness
And strength
And life.
No,
We couldn't do that—
Put your mind down.
Besides,
Your mind is stronger than you are
And won't let you,
You poor darling.

Yes,
Well,
If you hold out your hand
I'll take it.
But how,
My friend,
Might I hold your hand
If you keep it
Where I might not find it?

I possess—
I control—
I manipulate—
I lie—
I strive for power
for success
for fame
for immortality
for adoration
and
I play loving games
And
I try not to look like I'm doing
These things
Although
Well I know
Everyone else is doing them too,
Or making excuses—
But
I flaunt—
I preen—
I strut—
And sell
And horde
And steal the ideas of others.
I'm a machine
Designed for efficiency.

I'm you!

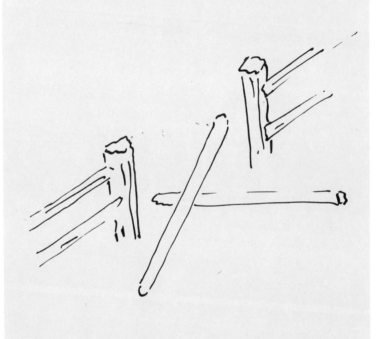

I'll play the game,
If you want to play
Your little game with me,
But just remember—
When it's over,
All the ox are free.

It was a grand Thanksgiving.
Loving friends came
And we spent the day,
And the night,
In warmth
And in softness
Amidst the laughing children
And along a valley stream
Walking,
And talking,
And thrilled by our communion.

We warmed by fires,
And we touched,
And we smiled at one another,
Often,
And we prayed,
I'm sure,
In whatever ways we pray,
To whatever we might pray to—
We prayed,
I'm sure,
That we would always
Have each other
And we would do these things again
And again,
And again.

Many times
I'm a third person,
Watching.
I don't know
Whether it's because
I don't understand
What's being said
Or whether
It's because I don't wish to,
But,
A third person
Watching
Is lonely,
Don't you know?
A third person
Watching
Is only watching.

I love a toad's belly
With his yellow-green-white
Skins
Pulsed with living.
I love a toad's belly
With his skin drawn as a drum
Across his stomach of bugs
And his heart of smiles.
I love to look into
A great toad's eyes
And note the smile
On his face,
His quite eternal smile,
Grow wider—
As I kiss him on his belly—
As I kiss her on her belly—
It makes no difference which;
All toads kiss the same.

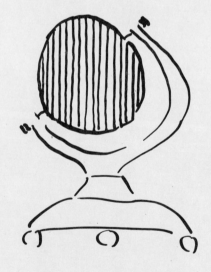

Take
Your funny little world
And stuff it
Up your ass.
I never asked you
For any advice.

A little girl,
Stars in her eyes,
Serious face,
And softing hand
On my leg
Said —
"Mr. Harger,
I mean Bill,
I like you
Because you're a good man."
Just a little girl,
And she probably
Changed my life.

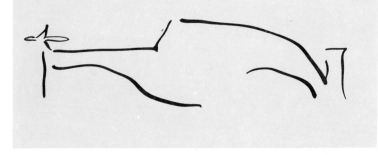

I know what I like
And . . . .
　　　I don't like it!

Oftentimes
I love someone
And when I do
I tell 'em.
So,
If I haven't told you dear,
I don't,
And it isn't because
You're not worthy
And it isn't because
I'm blind.
It's just that when I find
The folks
That I'm inclined to love
I check their instinct
For loving back,
If I should say I do,
And that's the problem
With you—
That's the reason I don't.
It's either because
I know you can't
Or because I know you won't.

I hope
You don't mind
That
I love you.

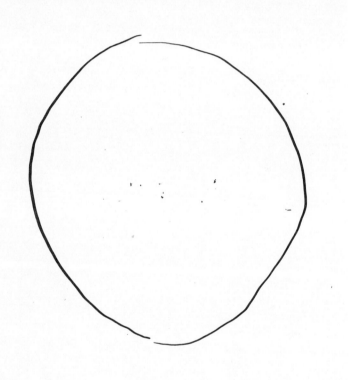

Being
Is knowing who you are
But not caring
If anybody else knows.
Being
Is happiness
Of such fulfillment
And delight
You need not display to others
Your happiness.
Being
Is soft and warm.
Being
Is creative,
And thoughtful,
And infinite.
Being
Is compassionate.
Being
Is everybody else knowing
Who you are,
What you are,
And your knowing they know,
And your not caring anyway.
Being
Is wonderful.
Being
Is!

The payment
For the workings of my mind
Is exhilaration
Or consternation
In the minds of others.
I do it everywhere I go.
I do it all the time.
And I really don't know what for.
I wonder
If my mind's a whore?

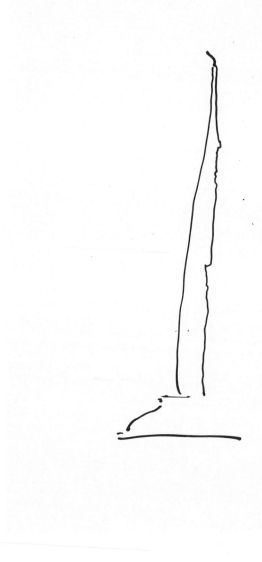

Sleep,
Take me.
I am yours
As I have been
No one's before.

Sleep,
Do with me
What you will.

There is a sweet smell
In the air . . . . .
There is a tune flying sweet

And I don't know
Why I can hear it
And no one else can!

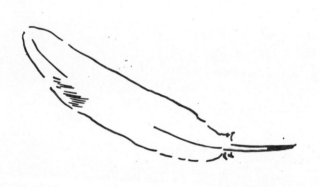

Stay happy
And soft
And stay yourself
And enjoy yourself
And give yourself
To others
But
Save some for yourself.

William Harger is an Aquarius and pretty much acts like one. He digs people and he loves life. When he must have privacy, he must have privacy. When he must have people, he must have people. He now lives in the wilderness of Trinity County, California, with a pixie wife, uncontrollably growing boys and wonderful seclusion. Getting there was a nice trip. Born in L. A. in 1936, raised between city life and grandma's farm, Bill graduated an aeronautical engineer and treadmilled it a while with many of his old friends. Fifteen years of drafting, grey suits, inventions, martinis, management, patents, Jaguar sedans, and "everything I've always wanted" blew him away to the mountains for a couple of years off. He never came back. Between lectures, reading to kids, taking troups into the woods, and a heavy stint in the environmental crisis talk circuit, he wrote. Poetry mostly, but anything really. He may sound tongue in cheek, but he probably isn't. He may sound too simple sometimes, but that's misleading. He sounds terribly philosophical at times and maybe he is. His art is used to express the things he's learned about himself and his place in nature. His message is the right to individuality . . . the beauty of me . . . pride in the only real gift we have to offer to the world about, the perfect uncoated, fearless "me." And, when you've finished his book, don't love him; love yourself. Bill is out to impress you with "YOU."

CELESTIAL ARTS BOOK LIBRARY:

SPECTRUM OF LOVE. Walter Rinder's remarkable love poem with magnificently enhancing drawings by David Mitchell. 64 pages. Clothbound, $5.95; Paperbound, $2.95.

LOVE IS AN ATTITUDE. The world-famous book of poetry and photographs by Walter Rinder. 128 pages. Clothbound, $5.95; Paperbound, $3.95.

THIS TIME CALLED LIFE. New poems and photographs by Walter Rinder. 160 pages. Clothbound, $5.95; Paperbound, $3.95.

VISIONS OF YOU. Poems by George Betts, with photographs by Robert Scales. 128 pages. Paperbound, $3.95.

MY GIFT TO YOU. New poems by George Betts, with photographs by Robert Scales. 128 pages. Paperbound, $3.95.

HOW CAN I SHOW THAT I LOVE YOU? New ways of love in photographs and text by Elisa Bowen. 128 pages. 8½ x 11 inches. Paperbound, $4.95.

CELEBRATION OF LIFE. A photographic rendering by Elisa Bowen of two stanzas from the Chinese poet-philosopher, Lao-Tze. 80 pages. Clothbound, $3.95; Paperbound, $2.50.

OPEN AS SKY. A provocative love story in photos and poetry by Elisa Bowen. 96 pages. Clothbound, $3.95; Paperbound, $2.50.

LET EVERYTHING THAT BREATHES. A sensitive message for the human spirit by Robert Fulton and Micha Langer. 64 pages. Paperbound, $2.95.

THE PEOPLE'S BOOK. A photo album of the new generation of Americans taken by John McCleary. 104 pages. 10 x 14 inches. Paperbound, $2.95.

THE HITCHHIKERS. A photo-documentary of experiences on American highways by Phil Wernig. 128 pages. Paperbound, $2.95.

THE SECRETS OF BELLY DANCING. The amazing ancient art made popular in photographs and text by Roman Balladine and Sula. 96 pages. Paperbound, $2.95.

GAMES STUDENTS PLAY (And what to do about them.) A study of Transactional Analysis in Schools, by Kenneth Ernst. 128 pages. Clothhound, $6.95; Paperbound, $3.95.

HOW TO DOUBLE YOUR TRAVEL FUNDS. Financed entirely by a small retirement check, the authors spanned the world. By Charles and Carolyn Planck. 144 pages. Clothbound, $6.95; Paperbound, $3.95.

I AM. Concepts of awareness in poetic form by Michael Grinder. Illustrated in color by Chantal. 64 pages. Paperbound, $2.95.

SPEAK THEN OF LOVE. Poetry from Andrew Oerke a former Peace Corps Director for Africa. 80 pages. Paperbound, $2.95.

YOU AND I. Poems and photographs by Leonard Nimoy, the distinguished actor. 96 pages. Clothbound, $5.95; Paperbound, $2.95.

ACROSS THE DARK. Witty, yet haunting poems and epigrams by Brett Brady. Illustrated in color. 144 pages. Paperbound, $3.95.

OF A POET. He may sound too simple sometimes, but that's misleading. Poems and illustrations by William Harger. 96 pages. Paperbound, $2.95.

CHAIRMAN MAO'S 4-MINUTE PHYSICAL FITNESS PLAN. China thinks thin and tough, now Americans can do the same. 64 pages. 7½ x 7½ inches. Record of original music included. Paperbound, $3.95.